E
DAVI   Davis, Lee

FEEDING TIME

DATE DUE	BORROWER'S NAME	ROOM NUMBER

5/01

A Note to Parents

Dorling Kindersley Readers is a compelling new program for beginning readers, designed in conjunction with leading literacy experts, including Dr. Linda Gambrell, Director of the School of Education at Clemson University. Dr. Gambrell has served on the Board of Directors of the International Reading Association and as President of the National Reading Conference.

Beautiful illustrations and superb full-color photographs combine with engaging, easy-to-read stories to offer a fresh approach to each subject in the series. Each *Dorling Kindersley Reader* is guaranteed to capture a child's interest while developing his or her reading skills, general knowledge, and love of reading.

The four levels of *Dorling Kindersley Readers* are aimed at different reading abilities, enabling you to choose the books that are exactly right for your child:

Level 1 – Beginning to read
Level 2 – Beginning to read alone
Level 3 – Reading alone
Level 4 – Proficient readers

The "normal" age at which a child begins to read can be anywhere from three to eight years old, so these levels are intended only as a general guideline.

No matter which level you select, you can be sure that you are helping your child learn to read, then read to learn!

Dorling [DK] Kindersley

LONDON, NEW YORK, SYDNEY, DELHI, PARIS,
MUNICH, and JOHANNESBURG

Project Editor Deborah Murrell
Art Editor Catherine Goldsmith
Senior Art Editor Clare Shedden
Managing Editor Bridget Gibbs
US Editor Regina Kahney
Senior DTP Designer
Bridget Roseberry
Production Shivani Pandey
Picture Librarian Diane Legrande
Picture Researcher Marie Osborn
Jacket Designer Karen Burgess
Natural History Consultant
Theresa Greenaway

Reading Consultant
Linda Gambrell, Ph.D.

First American Edition, 2001
00 01 02 03 04 05 10 9 8 7 6 5 4 3 2 1
Published in the United States by DK Publishing, Inc.
95 Madison Avenue, New York, New York 10016

Library of Congress Cataloging-in-Publication Data

Davis, Lee, 1941-
   Feeding Time / by Lee Davis. -- 1st American ed.
   p. cm. -- (Dorling Kindersley readers)
   ISBN 0-7894-7357-7 (pbk.) -- ISBN 0-7894-7358-5 (hc)
   1. Animals--Food--Juvenile literature. [1. Animals--Food habits.]
I. Title. II. Series.
QL756.5.D38 2001
599--dc21   00-056973

Color reproduction by Colourscan, Singapore
Printed and bound in China by L. Rex

The publisher would like to thank the following for their kind
permission to reproduce their photographs:
Key: t=top, b=bottom, l=left, r=right, c=center
Bruce Coleman Ltd: Dr. P. Evans 10-11. **Gables:** 4-5, 14-15, 20-21.
Robert Harding Picture Library: 8-9. **N.H.P.A.:** Martin Harvey 23.
Oxford Scientific Films: Edwin Sadd 24-25; Gerald Thompson 13;
Konrad Wothe 30-31; Michael Fogden 22l; Richard Packwood 6-7.
Planet Earth Pictures: M & C Denis-Huot Front Jacket; Thomas
Dressor Front Jacket; Jonathan P. Scott 21r. **Ian Redmond:** 18-19.

see our complete
catalog at
www.dk.com

![DK] DORLING KINDERSLEY *READERS*

BEGINNING
1
TO READ

Feeding Time

Written by Lee Davis

A Dorling Kindersley Book

It is morning.

The sun is rising.

Animals that eat in the daytime start to look for food.

A gorilla yawns in his nest.
He reaches out his hairy hand
to feel for a tasty plant.
He has breakfast in bed.

plant

A herd of elephants
is ready for breakfast, too.
The elephants wrap
their trunks around
clumps of grass.

They curl their trunks
to break off the grass
and put it in their mouths.

Another elephant snaps off
branches from a big tree.
He chews the bark
on each branch.

bark

A large elephant knows
there are some crunchy seed pods
in the tall trees.
He stretches his trunk
to reach them.

seed pods

Zebras reach down
to nibble the grass.

grass

They bite the grass
with their front teeth.

A giraffe with her long neck
can reach the tree tops.
She wraps her tongue around
the tasty, tender shoots.
Her tongue tears the shoots
off the branches.

shoots

banana

The elephants wander
through the forest.
They find some banana plants.
They shake the branches
to make the bananas fall off.

A rhino spends most of the day
eating grass.
An oxpecker clings to the rhino.

The oxpecker eats ticks
and insects on the rhino's skin.
He pecks at them
with his pointed beak.

tick

A chimpanzee is looking
for termites to eat.
He digs with a stick
into a huge termite hill.
He makes a large hole
in the termite hill
and the termites spill out.

termites

Elephants need to eat salt.
They do not get enough salt
in their food.
So they dig up
clumps of salt to eat.

A herd of buffalo
moves to the river
for a drink.
Crocodiles watch and wait.
They are as still as rocks.

Slowly, a crocodile
swims closer.
Can he grab
a young buffalo
for his dinner?

Hippos spend the hot day
in the water.

In the evening, the air is cooler.
So they come out
to eat the short grass
on the river banks.

As the sun sets,
the elephants enjoy
a late evening snack.

Maybe some more fruit
and then a long, cool drink!

Picture word list

plant
page 7

shoots
page 17

bark
page 10

banana
page 19

seed pods
page 12

tick
page 21

grass
page 14

termites
page 22